praise for *I want to start by saying*

In this gorgeous hybrid work, Samuel Ace tells and untells the story of a family for whom estrangement has become a tradition: "I want to start by saying who was passed over. By whom. / I want to start by saying what was the art I saw. I want to start by saying my home and the mess of it." Ace's careful hands fold and re-fold the known facts, weighing the pain of knowing against the risks of telling. "I want to start by saying that the history I learned in school had no bones," Ace writes, "I want to start by saying that the teachers at school did not talk to us about the city that was on fire. Like it wasn't our city. Or anyone's. Or that it didn't exist." *I want to start by saying* is an accumulative record made of the light from Tucson, the greens of New England, and the yard-forests and gravel pits of Cleveland. Ace's simmering, hesitant, protective attention works to bear the weight of secrets passed unsaid. **SARAH MINOR, AUTHOR OF** ***Slim Confessions: The Universe as A Spider or Spit***

Sam Ace takes on the phrase "I want to start" as metronome that turns daily reflections into mediations on longing and loss, memory and pleasure, luck, absence, and value… this book is trans at its core. It is homey, heartfelt, and utterly beautiful. **EMERSON WHITNEY, AUTHOR OF** ***Daddy Boy***

I want to

start by saying

I want to start by saying
FIRST EDITION

Printed in the United States of America
ISBN 979·8·9897084·0·6

DESIGN ≈ SEVY PEREZ
Text in Brandon Grotesque & Adobe Caslon Pro

This book is published by the

Cleveland State University Poetry Center
csupoetrycenter.com
2121 Euclid Avenue, Cleveland, Ohio 44115-2214

a CATALOG RECORD *for this* TITLE *is*
AVAILABLE *from the* LIBRARY OF CONGRESS

Although events in this book are based on true stories, this is a book of creative nonfiction. Some names, locations, and timelines have been altered for privacy and storytelling purposes, and do not necessarily reflect actual thoughts, feelings, or actions of any individual.

I want to start by saying

SAMUEL ACE

~~~

I want to start by saying I hear the filter in the turtle tank like a fountain.

I want to start by saying like a fountain in the middle of a field of wildflowers.

I want to start by saying that today would have been my father's 84th birthday,
that he died eighteen days before his 79th.

I want to start by saying that he was young and that death took him by surprise.

I want to start by saying that my mother died nine months ago, less than four
and a half years after my father.

I want to start by saying the beginning of this sentence.

I want to start by saying that a child could have been born in that time.

I want to start by saying that a whole year has gone by since my godchild's birth.
~~~

I want to start by saying on Canada Day.

I want to start by saying the fireworks on the porch of a former riverboat inn at Hatfield Point.

I want to start by saying the fireworks marked the day.

I want to start by saying I celebrate my godchild. Not the nation.

I want to start by saying my godchild now says *bird* and *boat.*

I want to start by saying that both my sisters have children who are mostly grown.

I want to start by saying I do not know them. The children.

I want to start by saying I knew them up until my niece was nine and my nephew was seven.

I want to start by saying when my nephew was two he discovered a raccoon while looking out the window of the house in Austerlitz. He pointed and said *coo coo* long before we could identify what he was seeing.

I want to start by saying it began to rain last night. It's now past noon the next day and still raining. Soft and constant, hidden under the sound of the water filter.

~~~

I want to start by saying that it's difficult to come to the page.

I want to start by saying that I can no longer find my father's last voice message.

I want to start by saying that today I read about a German soldier who destroyed a small French town toward the end of World War II.

I want to start by saying that the soldier tortured then killed nearly every person living in that town.

I want to start by saying that 75 years later he is just now being tried for murder.

I want to start by saying I want to call my father.

I want to start by saying his voice might still be alive on an old cell phone buried in a box somewhere in my closet.
~~~

I want to start by saying an archive.

I want to start by saying how to retrieve the past.

I want to start by saying there are so many versions.

I want to start by saying that my closet is filled with intentions. I feel them every morning when I take out my clothes, get dressed, and close the door.

I want to start by saying that the intentions are always waiting.

I want to start by saying that last night nine people were murdered at an AME church in Charleston.

I want to start by saying that yesterday US soldiers in Nevada, operating drones over Afghanistan, murdered a family of five.

I want to start by saying my father would have cried watching Obama sing "Amazing Grace."

I want to start by saying that I cried but what are tears.

I want to start by saying that I cry whenever I see a baby being born.

I want to start by saying on tv or in a movie.

I want to start by saying it feels like a deep and shredding grief.

I want to start by saying on tv.

I want to start by saying will I ever witness a baby being born.

I want to start by saying I want to hear my father's voice.

~~~

I want to start by saying that I think through my fingers, my shoulders, my eyes when they are closed.

I want to start by saying it's the movement of my hands on a keyboard that I love. Not the residue or the aftermath.

I want to start by saying not even the words.
~~~

~~~

I want to start by saying that somewhere I have just passed 730 words. Auspicious because 7 + 3 + 0 equals 10 equals 1. Which is a lucky number.

I want to start by saying that somewhere I have passed 3,561 characters. Auspicious because 3 + 5 + 6 + 1 equals 15 equals 6. Which is also a lucky number. I have checked.

I want to start by saying that when I pump gas or consider an address as a place to live, I want the total to equal 1, 3, 6, 9, 10, 11, or 12.

I want to start by saying that I constantly add numbers inside my head.

I want to start by asking if I should delete the first six words. They are probably unnecessary.

I want to start by saying that I'd like to hold onto them for a while. They are lucky.
~~~

~~~

I want to start by saying that I am in love with someone who has a chronic illness.

I want to start by saying that I research fecal transplants, pituitary gland tumors, Lyme disease, ME/CFS, antibiotics, immune boosters, immunosuppressants, anti-fungal agents, magnetic therapies, hormone deficiencies, gluten-free carbohydrates, ashwagandha, stevia, and Japanese knotweed.

I want to start by saying that this morning I advised my love to swallow his spit in order to strengthen his immune system.

I want to start by saying I need to stop giving advice.
~~~

~~~

I want to start by saying that I am not living in my home.

I want to start by saying that I have possessions in a small apartment in Tucson, Arizona. Also in a 5x5 indoor storage facility, also in Tucson. Also in my ex-wife's garage. Also piled inside a 9,000-square-foot warehouse in Truth or Consequences, New Mexico. I also have a small shelf of books, some files, an Aeropress coffee maker, two stainless-steel salad servers, a stainless-steel ladle, a nearly six-foot drawing I drew and gave to my parents for their anniversary almost 40 years ago, and a large gouache, painted by my mother, with vertical blue and black brushstrokes that seen together look something like a dancing woman.

I want to start by saying that several drawers of clothes are in Florence, Massachusetts, where I am now. The gouache and the drawing are all I have from my mother's last apartment.

I want to start by saying what is home.
~~~

~~~

I want to start by saying that my love is lying upstairs on a bed which is on
the floor of a bedroom-turned-office, squeezed between some shelves and
a desk, amid piles of books that are mostly not ours.

I want to start by saying that the walls are wrapped in cheerful yellow beadboard
and the branches of a large maple tree are visible through the one window
in the room.

I want to start by saying that we are not sleeping on the bed in the master
bedroom because something in that room makes my love nauseous,
and the too-soft mattress hurts my back.

I want to start by saying that my love dreams of returning west to live near
his family.

I want to start by saying that it's still raining.

I want to start by saying the green of New England hangs very heavy today.
~~~

I want to start by saying that I worry we will be moving to a house with a zip code that adds up to 16 and an address that adds up to 8.

I want to start by saying someone once told me that the number 16 is unlucky.

I want to start by saying that maybe it's not all bad because together the zip code and the street address add up to 24 which equals a 6, a good number.

I want to start by saying that this morning I looked at houses for sale in Hudson, New York, Chéticamp, Nova Scotia, and Tucson, Arizona.

I want to start by saying that the number 8 is sacred.

~~~

I want to start by saying I do not love being a caretaker.

I want to start by saying my eyes are open.

I want to start by saying that I miss him right now.

I want to start by saying I feel compelled.

I want to start by saying that I feel love, tenderness, worry. An ache.

I want to start by saying that I feel powerless and lonely.

I want to start by saying that tonight I will cook chicken soup with beets, celery, and carrots, and later I will help him bathe.
~~~

~~~

I want to start by saying that it rained again yesterday.

I want to start by saying that I could not sit still.

I want to start by saying there is no place to hide and the silence is maddening. I'm looking at an ironing board, a dead plant, a pile of unopened magazines, and Facebook, a scrapbook of the present that looks like the past. I'm looking at the cat staring out the front window. I'm looking at my hands, which look veiny and thin.

I want to start by saying that Guibert's *Ghost Image* is lying on the floor next to the bed, spine up and open to page 63 where I stopped reading at the point Guibert writes: *In a small cardboard box whose initial contents I no longer remember, I had gathered all the photographs taken of me since my infancy that I hadn't torn up.*

I want to start by saying I cannot open a bank account until the end of the month.

I want to start by saying I do not understand the next move.

I want to start by saying that my chest feels tight and it's hard to breathe.
~~~

~~~

I want to start by saying that yesterday was a lost day.

I want to start by saying that only my right foot is on the ground.
~~~

~~~

I want to start by saying that I have very little time.

I want to start by saying I hear the door open.

I want to start by saying my love has come home.

I want to start by saying I have a lot of time but I wait until the last minute to do anything.

I want to start by saying we are now lying down in bed. He is writing and I am writing.

I want to start by saying I would rather distract myself downstairs with the news or the cat.

I want to start by saying I will stay here, lying next to him in the silence.
~~~

~~~

I want to start by saying we are eating lunch with my sisters.

I want to start by saying that they look resigned. Or maybe sad.

I want to start by saying that it's the December after our mother's death. We are seated in a delicatessen in midtown New York. The other tables and the people at them all seem too close.

I want to start by saying that I've ordered a Caesar salad and my love has ordered a hamburger.

I want to start by saying that this is the first time I've seen my sisters since the funeral.

I want to start by saying that before our mother died, it had already been years.

I want to start by saying that my sisters are staring at my love.
~~~

I want to start by saying it's the first time they've met him.

I want to start by saying that one of my sisters is five years younger than me.
That between me and my other sister there is only a year and a half.

I want to start my saying that they believe I've betrayed the family.

I want to start by saying they also think I'm dating someone too young.

I want to start by saying I have no children and they each have two.

I want to start by saying what is harm.

I want to start by saying did I harm.

I want to start by saying my sisters fear me.

I want to start by saying they worry about what is to come. Like these sentences.

I want to start by saying I didn't think.

I want to start by saying I read and then there was applause.

I want to start by saying who have I helped.

I want to start by saying life or silence.

I want to start by saying could I ever be quiet.

I want to start by saying a spell inside my head, language I no longer own.

I want to start by saying my love looks younger than he is.

I want to start by saying that the sister closer to me in age looks anxious, as if she wants to get up from the table and leave.

I want to start by saying she begins to talk about her career and her husband who is ill with a slow-moving destruction. There is no cure and he still works. But how long.

I want to start by saying that since our mother's death my sister has not spoken to me. Except now at this lunch.

I want to start by saying I always liked her husband. Quiet and unassuming, he was always kind to me.

I want to start by saying that I take a bite of my salad but I am not hungry. My love has barely touched his hamburger.

I want to start by saying that the server asks if we need more water.

I want to start by saying that my sister would not talk to me even before our mother's death.

I want to start by saying that she has barely spoken to me for 30 years.

I want to start by saying that her sadness is familiar but I cannot say exactly what it is. Or can I.

I want to start by saying our mother's death.

I want to start by saying that no matter how successful or beautiful my sister was, our mother said no one would notice. All they would see was how she looked.

I want to start by saying that my sister told me this in tears at dinner one night when my niece was very young. That after a concert our mother yelled these words at her in the middle of the night. Over the phone.

I want to start by saying our mother's cruelty.

I want to start by saying was our mother drunk.

I want to start by saying my sister has always been beautiful.

I want to start by saying will she ever hear me say it.

I want to start by saying from childhood.

I want to start by saying that our mother force-fed me homemade eggnog.

I want to start by saying before bed because she thought I was too thin.

I want to start by saying too strange or boyish.

I want to start by saying that as a child I often refused to eat.

I want to start by saying our mother's diets.

I want to start by saying our mother always thought she was too fat. Her words.

I want to start by saying she was obsessed with how things looked. Too fat, too thin, too boyish for a girl, the wrong clothes, the wrong friends.

I want to start by saying my clothes, my weight, my sisters' weight, my mother's weight, my beard, my gender.

I want to start by saying I inherited my father's baldness.

I want to start by saying that unlike him, I do not have a comb-over.

I want to start by saying my mother would not be happy.

I want to start by saying that the first time she saw my moustache after I began my medical transition, she pointed to it and said *what's that?* and let out a grunt of disgust.

I want to start by saying that until that point she had refused to see me for almost seven years.

I want to start by saying that sometimes her voice still reprimands me.

I want to start by saying she acted as if her fears about what she believed others thought were true.

I want to start by saying my mother's obsessions.

I want to start by saying her husband and her houses.

I want to start by saying her daughters.

I want to start by saying marriage.

I want to start by saying family.

I want to start by saying Shaker Heights.

I want to start by saying perfect in what world.

I want to start by saying desire.

I want to start by saying my mother was an artist.

I want to start by saying should I say the word. Fat.

I want to start by saying do no harm.

I want to start by saying can I say.

I want to start by saying there are many versions of this story.

I want to start by saying what should be kept private.

I want to start by saying who is embarrassed.

I want to start by saying who am I protecting.

I want to start by saying what should be written.

I want to start by saying fiction.

I want to start by saying well, maybe.

I want to start by saying why write this at all.

I want to start by saying I might erase what's been written.

I want to start by saying if you are reading this.

I want to start by saying how shame has been passed through generations.

I want to start by saying humiliation.

I want to start by saying what I'm trying to say.

I want to start by saying I wanted to look like my father.

~~~

I want to start by saying my sister believes I do not care about the same things she cares about.

I want to start by saying something slightly different.

I want to start by saying I no longer feel sad about the same things. Or do I.

I want to start by saying my sister does not want to know.

I want to start by saying that her children are not allowed to speak to me.

I want to start by saying that her children obey.

I want to start by saying that I invited my younger sister to have coffee. At first she said yes, then wrote to say she couldn't make it.

I want to start by saying I stepped out of the family.
~~~

I want to start by saying they stepped away from me.

I want to start by saying if you are reading this.

~~~

I want to start by saying that I have recently turned 61 and my love has turned 35. It will be a good year because our numbers add up to 15 which adds up to 6, a multiple of 3, and a kind number.

I want to start by saying we were born in the same month.

I want to start by saying I often wonder if eventually he will fall for someone closer to his age.

I want to start by saying then what will I do.

I want to start by saying that I believe him when he says it's me he wants.

I want to start by saying that I believe him when he says he loves me.

I want to start by saying why do I need to know.
~~~

I want to start by saying will I change.

I want to start by saying will he.

I want to start by saying that I am lying next to him in bed.

I want to start by saying what is honesty.

I want to start by saying I am only a little afraid.

I want to start by saying I close my eyes and feel his fingers on my stomach.

I want to start by saying no. His hands have not moved from his laptop keyboard.

I want to start by saying I long for his fingers.

I want to start by saying is this a sign.

I want to start by saying I turn over.

I want to start by saying I look through a magazine and begin to read a story about a scooter. For a moment I want to buy one.

I want to start by saying then I think I will not buy one.

I want to start by saying I will not.

~~~

I want to start by saying that I write the beginning of this sentence in order to write this sentence.

I want to start by saying that this sentence is a subject.

I want to start by saying that sometimes I need words to be in the way.

I want to start by saying that I have taken out the beginning but I am back at the beginning.
~~~

~~~

I want to start by saying that I want to write away from my family.

I want to start by saying I keep writing about family.

I want to start by saying that the past is a rupture. No matter what I do.

I want to start by saying that indignity is such a dignified word. *Demean* feels closer to what happened.

I want to start by saying that I am suspicious of storytelling.

I want to start by saying that I am suspicious of self-pity.

I want to start by saying that I too am culpable.

I want to start by saying that I looked at my skin today and saw my age.
~~~

I want to start by saying my hairline has receded to the back of my head.
My beard and the hair around my ears, almost completely white.

I want to start by saying that I often do not believe I am getting older.

I want to start by saying that I am taking a walk.

I want to start by saying that I cannot identify which birds are singing this
morning. I wonder, is that a robin, a rose-breasted grosbeak, or a purple finch?

I want to start by saying that I am back to being bound up in love.

I want to start by saying I am avoiding the subject.

I want to start by saying that this morning I had to get up and walk downstairs
in order to hear myself.

I want to start by saying family.

I want to start by saying pause.

I want to start by saying my mother's death.

~~~

I want to start by saying that I sat quietly in a waiting room at the hospital where my father was dying. My mother and my two sisters sat in a different waiting room down the hall. They forbade me to join them.

I want to start by saying that I stared at the green flecked vinyl on the floor. It reminded me of the vinyl floor in my childhood dentist's office.

I want to start by saying that I sat next to my father's brother. He looked bloated and exhausted. He's closer in age to me than he was to my father.

I want to start by saying he told me he needed a scotch.

I want to start by saying that my father's father bullied his sons.

I want to start by saying I remember my grandfather saying *you are going to be a looker*.

I want to start by saying when I was four.
~~~

I want to start by saying *you look so sexy*.

I want to start by saying when I was six.

~~~

I want to start by saying that my father's sister died in the forties from a reaction to sulfa drugs. But maybe it was something else.

I want to start by saying that's the story I was told.

I want to start by saying she was eight years old.

I want to start by saying that my grandmother had a breakdown.

I want to start by saying that's the story I was told.

I want to start by saying that my grandfather committed my grandmother to an institution.

I want to start by saying or did her psychiatrist. Or did my grandmother herself.

I want to start by saying that after my grandfather died my grandmother was diagnosed with lung cancer. I traveled to Cleveland to be with her.
~~~

I want to start by saying I slept in my father's bedroom. Or had it become his brother's.

I want to start by saying I remember a desk built into a corner of the room. On the desk, a beige dial telephone and a small pad of paper embossed with the logo of my grandfather's construction company. Two single beds with small bookshelves for headboards.

I want to start by saying that in the center of the telephone's dial was a handwritten number that began with the letters *ye*.

I want to start by saying as if my father or his brother had never left.

I want to start by saying I found two volumes by Zane Grey on the shelves. Nothing else.

~~~

I want to start by saying that my grandmother and I sat in the den watching tv. She lay on the couch while I sat across from her in my grandfather's brown and plaid recliner.

I want to start by saying that my grandmother wore a nightgown and a soft pink robe.

I want to start by saying that she asked me about my book.

I want to start by saying my family would not speak to me because of it.

I want to start by saying as if what I wrote was truth.

I want to start by saying was it the truth.

I want to start by saying that my grandmother said there were things she would only ever tell her psychiatrist.
~~~

I want to start by saying what were those things.

I want to start by saying her father was a salesman and when she was young he would bring her with him on business trips.

I want to start by saying he would often visit his clients in local bars.

I want to start by saying my grandmother's eyes looked up at the ceiling as she talked.

I want to start by saying she told me her father would pick her up and put her on top of the tall bar counters where he would drink and show her off to his clients.

I want to start by saying that her story stopped there.

I want to start by saying I don't know what my great-grandfather was selling. I don't remember if my grandmother told me or not.

I want to start by saying that my grandfather was dead two years by the time we had this conversation.

I want to start by saying the shuffleboard painted on my grandparents' basement floor.

I want to start by saying the rubber shrunken head souvenirs in the storage closet. The black-and-white snapshots of horses and cacti from a Tucson vacation.

I want to start by saying I wanted to save my grandmother.

I want to start by saying her paintings of rabbis and clowns. Also in the basement.

I want to start by saying her yellow kitchen with one wall covered in a pattern of horse and buggy silhouettes.

~~~

I want to start by saying that I close my eyes and dream I am hiding something.

I want to start by saying I wake up.

I want to start by saying I am baffled that I'm living and traveling like a student.

I want to start by saying that even so, I'm afraid of losing everything.

I want to start by saying it's hot in this room.

I want to start by saying I can't fall back to sleep.
~~~

~~~

I want to start by saying that I've been out of the house twice today.

I want to start by saying that now I am sitting with a friend over coffee.
She mourns the loss of friends because she's in love with someone who is trans.

I want to start by saying the familiarity of so many stories.

I want to start by saying that I mourn the rise of rivers, the smell of creosote,
the relief of summer monsoons.
~~~

~~~

I want to start by saying that the dreams have not stopped, but this morning
    I do not remember them.

I want to start by saying that I feel like a planet covered with a veil.

I want to start by saying I am waiting for some news.

I want to start by saying that I want to get rid of the beginnings.

I want to start by saying that the beginning of the sentence is like a slide.
    A way to prepare.

I want to start by saying an easing in.

I want to start by pulling open the curtains.
~~~

I want to start by saying I'm afraid I don't know how to change the course of things.

I want to start by saying his body.

I want to start by saying I begin the day holding him.

I want to start by saying that I love the hair on his legs, his beard, his chest.

I want to start by saying that yesterday we had sex. Twice.

I want to start by saying once as we were falling asleep.

I want to start by saying that as I spooned him I began to trace the hair on his inner thighs, brushing his underwear just below his cock.

I want to start by saying that I went carefully as I knew he was tired, but he pushed against me, so I continued.

I want to start by saying it gave me pleasure to feel the quickening of his body,
the inevitable.

I want to start by saying I rested my hand between the crack of his ass and
his cock.

I want to start by saying I slept.

~~~

I want to start by saying where I came from.

I want to start by saying that I was a white child who grew up in the suburbs of Cleveland, Ohio. Until I was ten, my family lived in a small white house around the block from a Catholic college, surrounded by other small white houses and the white families who lived in them.

I want to start by saying there were many children and a small forest at the end of the block.

I want to start by saying I thought it was a forest.

Or was it a small tree-covered lot that seemed like one.I want to start by saying that last year I visited that street. The houses were still small, but the trees had grown tall.

I want to start by saying I first heard the word *schwartz* during Sunday morning brunch at my grandparents' house. I was five.
~~~

I want to start by saying that my father's father said the word.

I want to start by saying I also heard that word at Friday night dinners, as in *those schwartzes*, spoken by my mother's father as bits of stuffed cabbage and farfel fell out of his mouth.

I want to start by saying I wanted to throw up when I looked at my grandfather's mouth full of food.

I want to start by saying I had to leave the room to get away from the sound of his chewing.

I want to start by saying I still cannot bear the sound of chewing.

I want to start by saying I want to jump out of my skin.

I want to start by saying a cliché that perfectly describes the feeling.

I want to start by saying I cannot sit at the table when my love is eating.

I want to start by saying I only learned about misophonia a few years ago.

I want to start by saying that before I learned about misophonia, I believed something was wrong with me.

I want to start by saying knowledge did not make sitting at the table any easier.

I want to start by saying that the word *schwartz* in my grandfather's mouth meant the people who lived in the apartment building he owned downtown.

I want to start by saying that during those meals there were loud arguments.

I want to start by saying my sisters and I watched tv in the living room while our mother and her father argued.

I want to start by saying *Rawhide* or *Cheyenne*. Brach's marshmallow peanuts and red hots.

I want to start by saying we would leave my grandparents' house without finishing the show or saying goodbye.

~~~

I want to start by saying that in 1962 my mother filled the Buick station wagon with boxes of canned goods, medical supplies, a few toys, and suitcases full of clothing.

I want to start by saying that she planned to drive us to Canada when the missiles launched from Cuba.

I want to start by saying that she bought and filled two tall green metal cabinets with food.

I want to start by saying that she stored them in the basement near the old coal furnace.

I want to start by saying we were Jews.

I want to start by saying my mother's grandparents were murdered in the Holocaust.
~~~

I want to start by saying that when John F. Kennedy was murdered, my mother moved the tv up from the basement into the living room.

I want to start by saying she could not stop crying.

~~~

I want to start by saying my parents employed a gardener who worked at the house on Saturdays.

I want to start by saying that his name was Louis.

I want to start by saying that he pulled weeds and seemed very old. I was six when I met him but he did not talk to me.

I want to start by saying I never heard him say anything but *Yes Sir* and *Yes Ma'am* to my parents.

I want to start by saying that my father told me that Louis was from the south but I had no idea where that was.

I want to start by saying that during the week Louis worked for my father at the asphalt plant he managed on the Flats along the Cuyahoga River.

I want to start by saying that there were tall cone-shaped piles of gravel and dirt scattered around the plant.
~~~

I want to start by saying that three metal green cylinder-shaped silos rose up from the plant above the oily-dark river. Conveyor belts hung from the top of the silos, falling diagonally down toward the ground like roller-coaster tracks.

I want to start by saying that my father, the foreman B, and my father's secretary were white. Everyone else who worked at the plant was Black.

I want to start by saying that when I was six my father's parents moved to the country.

I want to start by saying at Sunday brunch my grandfather said they wanted to get away from downtown.

I want to start by saying what that meant.

I want to start by saying to live around white people.

I want to start by saying that when I was ten my family moved to a Tudor-style house in Shaker Heights, not far from downtown Cleveland.

I want to start by saying my grandparents did not approve. The house was too close to downtown.

I want to start by saying that my grandparents' new house sat on three acres of lawn.

I want to start by saying three large weeping willows stood close together in a shallow depression near the middle of the backyard. To help with drainage, my grandfather explained.

I want to start by saying that every person who lived on our new street in Shaker Heights was also white.

~~~

I want to start by saying 1964.

I want to start by saying that I believed 10 was the best age. I had finally arrived at 2 digits and 1 + 0 equals 1.

I want to start by saying that the brothers across the street played outside with their grandfather's rifle from World War II. The stock was made from honey-colored wood.

I want to start by saying I loved the sound of its metal bolt when it turned and clicked into place.

I want to start by saying that a black Ford Thunderbird with a porthole window sat in their driveway.

I want to start by saying the mansions at the end of the street backed up to a golf course.
~~~

I want to start by saying the sand traps on the golf course became trenches for our war games. The golfers were our enemies.

I want to start by saying that we got kicked off the golf course almost every time we played there.

I want to start by saying there was a rumor about the Van Sweringen brothers who built Shaker Heights.

I want to start by saying single beds in the same room.

I want to start by saying the brothers never married. I speculate.

I want to start by saying when they woke up in the morning did they share their dreams.

I want to start by saying that the van Sweringens wrote restrictive covenants into their plans.

I want to start by saying that in the fifties and sixties Jews and Blacks moved into Shaker Heights.

I want to start by saying that the press said they were welcomed.

I want to start by saying they were not welcomed.

I want to start by saying the language of my childhood. What was said around the dinner table.

I want to start by saying WASP.

I want to start by saying something specific.

I want to start by saying 3139 Montgomery Road. A bigger house than the one we moved from, but smaller compared to the mansions at the end of the street.

I want to start by saying another 16. Oh no.

I want to start by saying that the woman who cleaned my ex-wife's house told her that the number 16 is dangerous.

I want to start by saying my ex was superstitious.

I want to start by saying we shared certain beliefs.

I want to start by saying that when I was ten and a half, my mother forbade me to wear jeans or to play with the boys across the street.

~~~

I want to start by saying a website says *The City and its residents made national headlines in the 1950s when they reexamined years of restrictive covenants. . . .* Before that, no Jews no Blacks.

I want to start by saying that I attended Malvern School in Shaker Heights.

I want to start by saying in the 1970s: *Racial balance continued in Shaker Schools through a voluntary busing program.*

I want to start by saying that despite the claims of this public history, no one in my fourth-grade class was Black.

I want to start by saying when the Jews and Blacks moved in the WASPs moved out.

I want to start by saying dinner-table explanations.

I want to start by saying the remaining WASPs lived in the big houses at the end of the street. The houses that backed up to the golf course.
~~~

I want to start by saying we thought their backyards belonged to us.

I want to start by saying that I thought 3139 was an English Tudor but a real estate website says French Normandy. In the photos, the interior looks utterly changed. A redone kitchen, silk curtains, a closed-in porch. I hardly recognize any of it except for the placement of the couch in the den where I threw up the eggs my father tried to feed me one morning when I had the flu. Perhaps also the pachysandra beds my mother planted in the front yard.

I want to start by saying that today two years' worth of taxes equal what my parents paid for the house in 1963.

I want to start by saying I sometimes think about returning to Cleveland.

I want to start by saying the poets Russell Atkins and Julie Patton live there.

I want to start by saying that to get to school I walked two blocks and across South Woodland to the end of Montgomery Road.

I want to start by saying that one Sunday morning I decided to teach my younger sister to ride a bicycle without training wheels.

I want to start by saying that we took our Shetland sheepdog with us when we went outside.

I want to start by saying that his name was Beaver. Beaver was a year old and loved to herd everything, including his humans. Including cars.

I want to start by saying that when we were leaving the house I could not find a leash.

I want to start by saying that when we reached South Woodland, Beaver ran into the street to chase a car. Almost immediately he was hit.

I want to start by saying killed.

I want to start by saying the car stopped. A man got out and carried Beaver over to the sidewalk.

I want to start by saying I panicked and ran home to get someone.

I want to start by saying I left my little sister with Beaver and her bicycle on the sidewalk.

I want to start by saying that after Beaver died I could not cry.

I want to start by saying shame.

I want to start by saying horror.

I want to start by saying my mother in tears.

I want to start by saying she did not yell at me.

I want to start by saying I could not sleep.

I want to start by saying my parents brought me downstairs.

I want to start by saying that I sat on the floor in the living room.

I want to start by saying they sat above me on a couch with drinks. Vodka on ice.
Scotch on ice.

I could not look at them.

I could not cry.

~~~

I want to start by saying that the Hough neighborhood of Cleveland burned the July before I went to junior high school. A white bar owner had refused a Black customer a drink of water.

I want to start by saying that my mother began to talk about buying a gun.

I want to start by saying that my parents argued about this. Loudly and often.

I want to start by saying what if.

I want to start by saying like when she threw dishes against the wall.

I want to start by saying often.

I want to start by saying if she came after me.

I want to start by saying would she do it. Buy a gun.
~~~

I want to start by saying there were riots for weeks. Four people were killed, all of them Black.

~~~

I want to start by saying that when I was twelve the city was on fire.

I want to start by saying that the history I learned in school had no bones.

I want to start by saying that the teachers at school did not talk to us about the city that was on fire. Like it wasn't our city. Or anyone's. Or that it didn't exist.

I want to start by saying that every day we had French class.

I want to start by saying that when I lived in Shaker Heights, I often dreamt of dungeons and torture. I woke up sexually aroused.

I want to start by saying I smelled something rotting.
~~~

~~~

I want to start by saying the deep orange skies of the monsoon.

I want to start by saying we have returned to Tucson.

I want to start by saying that while our friends are away, we are taking care of their little house. Their dark rooms and heavy wood benches.

I want to start by saying I fall asleep in my love's arms.

I want to start by saying I think about waking up alone. I wonder if that might be the future.

I want to start by saying the yellow butterfly bush, the light magenta bougainvillea, and the deep red flowers on the barrel cactus.

I want to start by saying the smell of creosote.
~~~

I want to start by saying that at first our arrival felt dusty.

I want to start by saying the desire to buy a house on the second day.

I want to start by saying that my friend S told me my boyfriend looked like Jesus.

I want to start by saying I found a Jesus on a prayer card at the Mission.

I want to start by saying that the Jesus on the prayer card was white and very thin with long blonde hair and a blonde beard.

I want to start by saying that my love does resemble the prayer-card Jesus.

I want to start by saying gay Jesus.

I want to start by saying that at the Mission I also found an 8.5x11-inch holographic portrait of Jesus and Mary.

I want to start by saying that tilting the card one way shows Jesus.

I want to start by saying that tilting the card the other way shows Mary.

I want to start by saying that holding the card steady in the middle shows Jesus and Mary merged together.

I want to start by saying trans Jesus. Trans Mary.

~~~

I want to start by saying that instead of meeting me for coffee my younger sister tells me she will send me a second payment from my mother's estate.

I want to start by saying 20 percent.

I want to start by saying that my sisters each received 40 percent.

I want to start by saying how did they decide.

I want to start by saying that I have not seen the terms of probate.

I want to start by saying that my father died five years ago last month and I never saw my father's will.

I want to start by saying that when I asked, my sister's lawyer sent me a will from 1997 in which I was disowned.
~~~

I want to start by saying that the year before my father died he called to ask for my current address and social security number as he was rewriting his will.

I want to start by saying that the new will mysteriously disappeared.

I want to start by saying that my father and I talked on the phone every week or every other week.

I want to start by saying for hours.

I want to start by saying that my father kept secrets.

I want to start by saying that the 2,700 miles between us was often a convenience of distance.

I want to start by saying that our conversations were intimate. Also a convenience of distance.

I want to start by saying that while my father was dying, his brother told me that he thought it was my choice to never again see or speak to my parents or my sisters.

I want to start by saying he thought I had chosen to disappear.

I want to start by saying my parents led him to believe that story.

I want to start by saying there were no pictures of me in my parents' apartment.

I want to start by saying that I accepted the conditions of my father's love.

I want to start by saying I was frightened to upset the balance of our connection.

I want to start by saying that what he shared with me in private seemed more real than how he lived.

I want to start by saying more real to both of us.

I want start by saying that his fear of my mother's fury was just as real.

I want to start by saying I am more like him than I often care to admit.

~~~

I want to start by saying that we are still at our friends' house.

I want to start by saying that the coved ceilings have no visible corners and look like the sky.

I want to start by saying that a dusky deep beige fills the sky that is the ceiling.

I want to start by saying I am sitting in a chair, staring at the backyard.

I want to start by saying my love is making breakfast in the kitchen.

I want to start by saying I am mistaken.

I want to start by saying so much time.
~~~

~~~

I want to start by saying that scientists can now turn skin cells into eggs and sperm.

I want to start by saying I love the thick hair on my love's chest, his in-between.
    I love his thoughtful quiet and his long thin legs.

I want to start by saying that I love the possibility of our child.

I want to start by saying that I want a child that comes from both of us.

I want to start by saying we decide to inseminate.

I want to start by saying we are shopping.
~~~

~~~

I want to start by saying that yesterday we drove from Chicago to Cleveland.

I want to start by saying that yesterday was my parents' anniversary.

I want to start by saying that we are staying at Julie Patton's high up in the trees. With Janice Lowe and RJ. Paul and Nhojj.

I want to start by saying that Julie's house is many houses. A tall brick building that once held several apartments.

I want to start by saying that Julie and I both grew up in Cleveland.

I want to start by saying that last night we all read to each other. Or sang.

I want to start by saying that we woke up to sirens racing down East Boulevard.

I want to start by saying Rockefeller Park and Glenville.
~~~

I want to start by saying the lake a far ocean.

I want to start by saying that Cleveland smells like home. Like rust and dirt and fallen leaves.

I want to start by saying that Julie and I did not meet until we both lived in New York.

I want to start by saying that Julie's mother was a painter. So was my mother.

I want to start by saying that my mother's art did not know Julie's mother's art.

I want to start by saying who is a mother.

~~~

I want to start by saying the large rooms of the apartment building on East Boulevard.

I want to start by saying the fields outside Julie's window. The gardens and the farms.

I want to start by saying deep summer. Art filling every room.

I want to start by saying Virgie Ezelle Patton, Julie's mother.

I want to start by saying the building ghosts then and now.

I want to start by saying the cars and the sirens.

I want to start by saying the boiler.

I want to start by saying Virgie and her paintings.
~~~

I want to start by saying I did not know her.

I want to start by saying my mother's aspirations.

I want to start by saying she took us to museums. Art and natural history.

I want to start by saying a yearly subscription to Severance Hall and the symphony.

I want to start by saying the Cleveland Institute of Art just down the street from
 the Cleveland Institute of Music. All the institutes.

I want to start by saying theory lessons beginning at four years old.

I want to start by saying did they know each other. My mother and Virgie.

I want to start by saying I know so little.

I want to start by saying my great-grandparents were Jews from Minsk.
 Or was it Vilna.

I want to start by saying the boats they came on.

I want to start by saying I'm not sure. What is my memory.

I want to start by saying a woman in a sheer white nightgown. My father's grandmother floating through dark rooms. Diaphanous curtains. Possibly in one of those apartments on East Boulevard.

I want to start by saying I can no longer ask my mother. Or my father.

I want to start by saying what am I trying to say.

I want to start by saying that my mother bought whole shelves of large coffee-table art books.

I want to start by saying I long to know her.

I want to start by saying she too was a child of Eastern European immigrants. First generation American.

I want to start by saying she tried to give us something she did not have.

I want to start by saying she made my father throw away his jazz collection.

I want to start by saying an assumption of culture. White European.
Classical music and the bones of indigenous peoples in the museum.

I want to start by saying that the thought of running out of money terrified her.

I want to start by saying that even so, we moved often. Into bigger and
bigger houses.

I want to start by saying am I still a child, wandering through those rooms.

I want to start by saying but at whose house. Julie's or my mother's.

I want to start by saying that sometimes I want to go back. To see but not stay.

I want to start by saying a bronze sculpture on a tall white pedestal. My mother's.

I want to start by saying the orange and the red bodies of Virgie's women warm
on the walls.

I want to start by saying the blank faces of museum curators.

I want to start by saying who gets to choose. Who chooses.

I want to start by saying that outside Julie's house we walk through fields.

I want to start by saying how green and how wild.

I want to start by saying the wind.

I want to start by saying who am I in this.

I want to start by saying a daughter. Or a son.

I want to start by saying my mother wanted to be noticed.

I want to start by saying who was passed over. By whom.

I want to start by saying the art I saw.

I want to start by saying who made the art I did not see.

I want to start by saying my home and the mess of it.

I want to start by saying that in all her houses, my mother wanted to protect the polished wood floors.

I want to start by saying there was always paint on my clothes and on the floor of my room.

I want to start by saying I could not contain myself.

I want to start by saying I was watched.

I want to start by saying there was always someone to clean up. To put things back in order.

I want to start by saying I can still hear my mother shouting *do you ever learn.*

I want to start by saying the white walls of a gallery.

I want to start by saying what is the aspiration of white walls. Whose.

I want to start by saying my mother could make a beautiful room.

I want to start by saying that we went to the same museums. Julie and I.

I want to start by saying where do paintings get made. For that matter, words.

I want to start by saying Virgie and my mother shared at least one institute.

I want to start by saying what did it mean to each of them.

I want to start by saying where am I now.

I want to start by saying I need to make a phone call.

I want to start by saying the smell of leaves.

I want to start by saying what fits on the velvet green walls of the museum.

I want to start by saying preserved.

I want to start by saying whose legacy.

I want to start by saying the bones of someone's mother in the natural history
museum on University Circle.

I want to start by saying my mother scraped the layers of paint off all the
woodwork every time she moved.

I want to start by saying that after her death most of my mother's paintings were
stored and hidden away.

I want to start by saying who gets seen.

I want to start by saying that when she applied to art school my mother had three young children. She was told by admissions they didn't want housewives.

I want to start by saying did they take classes together. Two women. One Black, one white.

I want to start by saying the men in the corridors with paint on their pants.

I want to start by saying they were allowed.

I want to start by saying the smell of turpentine.

I want to start by saying the residue.

I want to start by saying whose models, whose version of art history.

I want to start by saying I aspire to mess.

I want to start by saying that today the mess is in this bed.

I want to start by saying I am trying to write it all down.

I want to start by saying will I ever leave my mother's aspirations behind.

I want to start by saying leave the dust.

I want to start by saying what is left of that building. The art institute.

I want to start by saying the circular hand-washing stations, the photo labs,
    the dark hallways now under a grassy field.

I want to start by saying where do we hang the mothers' paintings.

I want to start by saying who taught us about beauty.

I want to start by saying I smell rust.

I want to start by saying I smell Cleveland.

I want to start by saying Julie's rooms on East Boulevard.

I want to start by saying just down the road, half-draped models lay surrounded by easels. Window-lit.

I want to start by saying all of the rooms and what they held.

I want to start by saying the buildings stand, still there and not, in silhouette against the dark earth. The lake and the dirt.

I want to start by saying thank you.

~~~

I want to start by saying that we are back in Florence, Massachusetts.

I want to start by saying that it's 11 a.m. in the Robert Seydel Reading Room at Hampshire College.

I want to start by saying I imagined this room to be private and dark, with an entrance, a door, a fireplace, and some chairs, but the room is more like a pass-through, open for anyone on their way to somewhere else.

I want to start by saying that the two boys sitting behind me are having a loud conversation.

I want to start by saying *this is a reading room.*

I want to start by saying they stare at me for a long minute then leave.

I want to start by saying that I sit down and read Mac Low and Horn.
~~~

I want to start by saying the stories in Horn's book were collected by someone hired to collect stories.

I want to start by saying I skim through Burckhardt, Hujar, Thek, Johnson (Ray), Waldrop (Rosmarie and Keith), Wojnarowicz, Mueller, Gysin, de Kooning, and Pollock.

I want to start by saying *Ghost Tantras* by McClure.

I've made it! McClure says. *Here is total acceptance and god-belief wrapped in one hagreeow grahar.*

I want to start by saying so many sounds.

I want to start by saying words as physical objects.

I want to start by saying that the books here are mostly by men, and they are only a fraction of Seydel's collection.

I want to start by saying the books roar.

I want to start by saying the paint is thick.

I want to start by saying that I walk out into the heavy wet air of a dark campus.

I want to start by saying green.

I want to start by saying moss and birds.

I want to start by saying the benches outside are covered with burnt orange
Sunbrella.

I want to start by saying the benches are the same color as my mother's burnt
orange Naugahyde couch.

I want to start by saying my mother's kitchen.

I want to start by saying burnt orange wallpaper and burnt orange cushions on
Saarinen chairs.

I want to start by saying I can trace my mother's taste on a path through Danish Modern into the pages of the Knoll catalogue. Mine too.

I want to start by saying there were no family photos on the walls of the houses I grew up in. No family heirlooms visible in any room.

I want to start by saying that changed when the grandchildren were born.

I want to start by saying my father's Eames lounge chair, one of only two things I asked for after he died. The other was his watch.

I want to start by saying the chair was already spoken for.

I want to start by saying it was hard in the end.

~~~

I want to start by saying that my love's yawn used to scare me.

I want to start by saying not so much the yawn but the loud yell that followed.

I want to start by saying what I didn't say.

I want to start by saying I wonder if he can breathe.

I want to start by saying that when he yawns I think he's bored or distracted.

I want to start by saying with me.

I want to start by saying don't take it personally.

I want to start by saying how many people have said that to me.
~~~

I want to start by saying how watchful I am.

I want to start by saying that he yawns a lot.

~~~

I want to start by saying I hear the phone but do not answer.

I want to start by saying that the call is from one of my sisters.

I want to start by saying I think one of my sisters wants to tell me something
I do not want to hear.

I want to start by saying here we are again.

I want to start by saying what comes next.

I want to start by saying I have criminals in my family.

I want to start by saying I want to name names.

I want to start by saying will I.
~~~

I want to start by saying that the doors of silence are solid, heavy,
and lawyered up.

~~~

I want to start by saying that I write a letter to my sisters that I do not send.

I want to start by saying I pick my love up at the university so we can buy tickets to see the Dalai Lama.

I want to start by saying that the line is too long and we decide not to wait.

I want to start by saying that the Dalai Lama cancels anyway.
~~~

~~~

I want to start by saying that later in the day I walk up a steep hill in Amherst.

I want to start by saying I feel better afterwards. I run into a friend and we talk about partnerships and love. While we talk, two white boys speed by in a blue BMW. Blasting hip-hop.

I want to start by saying that another boy passes me on the sidewalk walking fast. His sweatshirt says K A N S A S in big white letters.
~~~

~~~

I want to start by saying again that only one of my sisters talks to me.

I want to start by saying that the other sister is silent.

I want to start by saying that I suspect they both have constructed a nearly indestructible narrative about me. They function as a bloc.

I want to start by saying for decades.

I want to start by saying that during our phone call my sister says she is thoroughly surprised I want to bring my love to the unveiling.

I want to start by repeating all of the italics.

I want to start by saying *it would only call attention to you.*

I want to start by saying *if you bring him, the ceremony would be about you, not about our mother.*
~~~

I want to start by saying *no one, not one person, wants him to come.*

I want to start by saying that after our father's funeral I was asked to leave.

I want to start by saying *it was just too much. You are just too much.*

I want to start by saying the day our father died.

I want to start by saying *we are having a gathering at the house, but you are not invited.*

I want to start by saying *you have always been selfish.*

I want to start by saying *if you bring him it will be more about you than our father.*

I want to start by saying because the book.

I want to start by saying *you might make up something sexual about our children. You are not to be trusted.*

I want to start by saying *you can never see them.*

I want to start by repeating what has been said.

I want to start by saying my father made amends to me.

I want to start by saying how many times we had lunch. Just the two of us.

I want to start by saying the last time we had lunch I met him at his office and he introduced me to his colleagues as his son.

I want to start by saying he told me he did not want my sisters to reconnect with me only on his deathbed. I told him I had tried. Many times. He said he was trying too.

I want to start by saying he wanted something he did not live to see.

~~~

I want to start by saying I make the decision to go.

I want to start by saying my love did not join me.

I want to start by saying a gathering at a house on Long Island that belongs to friends of my parents. The house is full of art.

I want to start by saying a fireplace surrounded by white marble.

I want to start by saying Ellsworth Kelly plant drawings.

I want to start by saying Christopher Wool.

I want to start by saying that my sister sits on the floor next to our cousin.
~~~

I want to start by saying my sister looks at me and says I was always the prettiest.

I want to start by saying that like my father I am going bald.

I want to start by saying I shave my head.

I want to start by saying I shaved my head in the eighties, the nineties, the two
thousands, and now.

I want to start by saying that Long Island was cold.

I want to start by saying that I always wear a hat.

I want to start by saying that maybe, like my father, I want to hide my balding head.

I want to start by saying from the cold and from the heat.

I want to start by saying my father was famous for giving toasts.

I want to start by saying Jack Daniel's.

I want to start by saying that at this gathering every friend and relative shares a story about drinking with my parents.

I want to start by saying that my sisters' children seem full of dread.

I want to start by saying I wonder about the end of time.

I want to start by saying *work is life and life is work.*

I want to start by saying it is my sister who tells me this.

~~~

I want to start by saying my love cries when I return. He tells me I always seem to be OK.

I want to start by saying that I endure. Which is not the same.

I want to start by saying he wants me to show more emotion.

I want to start by saying like when my dog was killed on South Woodland.

I want to start by saying that I sleep holding him.

I want to start by saying that my body takes a long time to come.

I want to start by saying my numbness in the face of my family is ancient.

I want to start by saying that he gives me more than I acknowledge. I need to let him know.
~~~

~~~

I want to start by saying that he is yawning again but this time quietly.

I want to start by saying the bedsprings.

I want to start by saying I close my eyes.

I want to start by saying the gardens are starting to decay.

I want to start by saying that I can see the ruins.

I want to start by saying the baby we talk about.

I want to start by remembering how to draw.

I want to start by saying air hunger.
~~~

~~~

I want to start by saying two weeks since I last wrote.

I want to start by saying that during that time I drove 2,800 miles.

I want to start by saying I am in Tucson, staying with my friend in the deep beige house. I am lying down in the back room off the kitchen. I did not sleep well.

I want to start by saying that I can hear my friend's and his daughter's footsteps.

I want to start by saying I began my trip in Haydenville, Massachusetts, then drove to New York to celebrate Eileen's collected. I left early the next morning and drove to Cleveland.

I want to start by saying that each of my parents has one sibling who is still alive.

I want to start by saying they both live in Cleveland but hardly know each other.
~~~

I want to start by saying I visited each of them.

I want to start by saying my father's brother always offers me a scotch.

I want to start by saying I always decline.

I want to start by saying *oh you really are not one of us.*

I want to start by saying that my mother did not speak to her mother for many years before her mother's death.

I want to start by saying that my mother and her sister also did not speak for many years.

I want to start by saying they were not speaking when my mother died.

I want to start by saying it's a family tradition.

I want to start by saying that I called to tell my mother's sister about her sister's death.

I want to start by saying that after Cleveland I drove to Columbus to see my cousins.

I want to start by saying that I've always wanted them to speak up.

I want to start by saying their silence devastates me.

I want to start by saying I'm still ashamed to say it.

I want to start by saying that after Columbus it was a long drive to Tulsa where I slept in a dusty room.

I want to start by saying the temperature had reached the high 90s by the time I got to Texas.

I want to start by saying that the desert won't let me go.

I want to start by saying the dust.

I want to start by saying dust.

~~~

I want to start by saying that last night I slept in the new house for the first time. The house we bought in Tucson.

I want to start by saying I am here. Alone on a borrowed bed. It is 7 a.m. and the light is muted and white.

I want to start by saying that the bedroom is very large and I am looking up at the high ceiling.

I want to start by saying I feel calm.

I want to start by saying the soft white feels like a monk's room.

I want to start by saying the quiet suits me.

I want to start by saying that we miss each other but we are far away.
~~~

I want to start by saying that the room is porous to the outside.

I want to start by saying I am honored by the quiet coos of the white-winged
doves who rest in the mesquite tree.

I want to start by saying I want nothing on the walls.

~~~

I want to start by saying that when I arrive in Haydenville my love is asleep in our bed.

I want to start by saying he is a gender of his own.

I want to start by saying that everyone has a gender of their own.

I want to start by saying I can't stop looking at his face.

I want to start by saying that I am short and my ribs are like the skeleton of an ancient pterodactyl.

I want to start by saying that his legs are covered in thick hair that grows up around his knees and across his thighs.
~~~

I want to start by saying that it fades before rounding his ass.

I want to start by saying fecund.

I want to start by saying thickness and abundance somewhere red.

I want to start by saying somewhere dark.

I want to start by saying around his sex.

I want to start by saying my hands fit into the small of his back.

I want to start by saying his fingers are longer but thinner than mine.

I want to start by saying his red-brown beard.

I want to start by saying untrimmed and thick.

I want to start by saying the earth around his lips.

I want to start by saying his cheekbones from some Romanian mountain.

I want to start by saying my body a mirror.

I want to start by saying my nearly hairless legs.

I want to start by saying my pubic hair beginning to gray.

I want to start by saying my cock thicker but dryer with age.

I want to start by saying my waist more defined.

I want to start by saying the hair on my shoulders.

I want to start by saying my coarse beard and my neck a promontory.

I want to start by saying my thinning hair.

I want to start by saying my skin weathered from the sun.

I want to start by saying these are our bodies.

I want to start by saying the light in his cheeks, his sleeping chest.

I want to start by saying that one day he may be angry that I've written these things.

I want to start by saying do I objectify him.

I want to start by saying a beauty of his own.

I want to start by saying I want a record.

~~~

I want to start by saying Thanksgiving with 30 people we barely know. We are now living with a woman and her two children.

I want to start by saying the children are a farm, all genders, unimpeded.

I want to start by saying that whoopee cushions are a thing.

I want to start by saying that the other gay guest, male, looks warily at us.

I want to start by saying we stand in a circle and everyone is asked to introduce themselves and say their pronouns.

I want to start by saying it feels like a performance.

I want to start by saying that after we leave, my love begins to cry.

I want to start by saying hold on, please don't go.
~~~

~~~

I want to start by saying I have monocular vision.

I want to start by saying the trees stand up like deep marks on the frozen air of the forest.

I want to start by saying every landscape reads like a painting.

I want to start by saying as a young child I wore prisms in my glasses to force my eyes to work together.

I want to start by saying it never worked.

I want to start by saying my left eye wanders.

I want to start by saying my left eye scans the perimeters. It watches and thinks while my right eye is busy seeing.
~~~

I want to start by saying I have no depth perception.

I want to start by saying that I possess a built-in translator of a translation.

I want to start by saying that for the first time I have no worries about money.

I want to start by saying when I wrote the previous sentence, I spit over my shoulder and said *kneina hura* to ward off the evil eye.

I want to start by saying I am happy on the road.

I want to start by saying I wrote this some days ago and then came the dreams.

I want to start by saying that in my dreams two men sit down to talk on the phone.

I want to start by saying there is also a she and there is a studio.

I want to start by saying that she is sewing while the chairs are wiped down by a scholarship student.

I want to start by saying that the men continue to talk.

I want to start by saying that the men might be contagious.

I want to start by saying that she is using a pink disinfectant and in the dream
I wish she'd spray it on the men.

I want to start by saying the steps go up to the balconies where three boys are
climbing down the side of the building.

I want to start by saying that my anger and my love feel like a part of everyone
in the dream.

I want to start by saying I run through a museum.

I want to start by saying the last twenty minutes when there is no fee and
it is free.

I want to start by saying I hear the sound of my feet and the breathing of
the guards.

I want to start by saying I notice the color of the walls but not anything hanging on them. Teal green and charcoal gray.

I want to start by saying a parquet floor.

I want to start by saying I suddenly notice a painting of a musty dog.

I want to start by saying the sounds.

~~~

I want to start by saying that it's now December.

I want to start by saying I try to start a fire.

I want to start by saying that the fire catches then goes out.

I want to start by saying that I need to say the beginning so I can hear the end.
~~~

~~~

I want to start by saying that two years ago I was alone in Truth or Consequences.

I want to start by saying that my marriage had fallen apart and my heart was broken.

I want to start by saying I celebrated the New Year at Passion Pie, dancing with the gay boys.

I want to start by saying that afterwards I took a walk with Wendy. She asked what was next and I did not know what to say.

I want to start by saying Paris.

I want to start by saying I was terrified to return to Tucson. When I left Truth or Consequences, I looked back before I locked the door.
~~~

I want to start by saying that now I am in the east, listening to a December rain.

I want to start by saying it falls softly and my love sleeps upstairs, as do the children and their mother.

~~~

I want to start by saying that the minutes are finally just minutes.

I want to start by saying the fifteen I began with are now gone.

I want to start by saying that the room is already full of people.

I want to start by saying the deadline is today and the deadline may be past.

I want to start by saying that the new house will be a workshop.

I want to start by saying that we cover the floor with heavy paper.

I want to start by saying the living room becomes a studio. There are tables for drawings and other tables for photographs.

I want to start by saying every thought turns into gesture.
~~~

~~~

I want to start by saying that we are visiting my love's parents.

I want to start by saying he grew up in this house.

I want to start by saying his mother is with me in the family room.

I want to start by saying that both he and his mother are my distant cousins.

I want to start by saying that his father thinks the government is watching us.

I want to start by saying that I think his father is partially right.

I want to start by saying the corporations more than the government.

I want to start by saying that his father tries to give me lessons in composting
and survival.
~~~

I want to start by saying that before we go to bed, his father tells me to buy a gun.

I want to start by asking if the gun would protect me.

I want to start by saying his father does not hear my sarcasm. He replies *well yes. Arizona. From hordes of people coming across the border.*

I want to start by saying I haven't seen anyone. I am tired and don't want to fight.

I want to start by saying where did you see that.

I want to start by saying *it's all over the news.*

I want to start by saying that he points to the 60-inch tv across the room.

I want to start by saying no one has come to my door or walked down my street.

I want to start by saying if they did I would give them food and water.

I want to start by saying I walk upstairs without saying goodnight.

~~~

I want to start by saying I hear screams.

I want to start by saying when we visit the tar pits.

I want to start by saying this was my father's business. The business of asphalt.

I want to start by saying a truck drove off a cliff at my father's plant and someone died.

I want to start by saying that there was always a crisis.

I want to start by saying like a truck driving off a cliff.

I want to start by saying or it rained all summer.

I want to start by saying or a worker fell into a vat of hot tar.
~~~

I want to start by saying or losing a home.

I want to start by saying or alcohol and raging fights in the night.

I want to start by saying or millions of dollars lost on a burning staircase.

I want to start by saying or bankruptcy.

I want to start by saying or a lawsuit.

I want to start by saying animals stuck in the tar and unable to get out.

I want to start by saying suffocation and the stink of oil.

I want to start by saying malevolence.

I want to start by saying the sacred ground of sacred bones.

I want to start by saying layers of dirt caked over by grasses.

~~~

I want to start by saying my love's body this morning.

I want to start by saying his hair in my mouth.

I want to start by saying he cradles me.

I want to start by saying his hand against my thigh and the planes overhead.

I want to start by saying how are you gone, dear C.D.

I want to start by saying Bryn too.

I want to start by saying goodbye.

I want to start by saying my 60s are treacherous.

I want to start by saying to my gorgeous friends: please stay alive.
~~~

~~~

I want to start by saying the heat and the room above our heads. The morning light on the walls.

I want to start by saying I thought we would have photographs. The planes from the airbase fly fast and loud.

I want to start by screaming the drones the drones.
~~~

~~~

I want to start by saying there's a party in the dark at the little community where I used to live.

I want to start by saying I look out over the pool at my old casita. I lived there for a year and a half when I separated from my wife.

I want to start by saying when I moved here I was sad.

I want to start by saying my little casita was dark and small. Like a cave.

I want to start by saying I felt comforted.

I want to start by saying my ex was unpredictable.

I want to start by saying I never knew what she might do.

I want to start by saying there were times I feared for my life.
~~~

I want to start by saying that the rent covered cable tv. I wrote a book to the accompaniment of many shows. *Sons of Anarchy*. Volume turned down.

I want to start by saying my dog Jack lived with me.

I want to start by saying the chatter across the blue carpet.

I want to start by saying that in the middle of the day I often drove back to my little casita from work to eat lunch and to take care of my dog.

I want to start by saying that Jack was blind.

I want to start by saying that I was eating lunch in the courtyard and TC was writing by the pool. Jack was lying at my side, but then wandered off. Blind, he got too close to the edge of the pool and fell into the water.

I want to start by saying that before I knew what was happening, TC jumped into the pool and pulled Jack out.

I want to start by saying that Jack had thick long hair and he weighed a hundred pounds.

I want to start by saying thank you.

I want to start by saying then every night *The Voice*, the alcohol, the hot tub.

I want to start by saying that I was often the only non-drinker soaking in a pool of drinkers.

I want to start by saying I wondered if I would eventually be banished.

I want to start by saying like by a family of drinkers.

I want to start by saying who do I trust.

I want to start by saying what happened Saturday.

I want to start by saying the night felt familiar.

I want to start by saying there was so much bamboo.

I want to start by saying the sound could have been chalk.

I want to start by saying my head is an uproar.

I want to start by saying I am deranged by sound.

~~~

I want to start by saying self-storage.

I want to start by saying that the planes from the airbase fly so low.

I want to start by saying the heart's storage.

I want to start by saying the years.

I want to start by saying baby.

I want to start by saying where is he.

I want to start by saying weather.

I want to start by saying family.
~~~

~~~

I want to start by saying water. Light and trees.

I want to start by saying that I am looking up.

I want to start by saying the slight shadows from the high windows.

I want to start by saying that my godchild and her mother came over for a visit.

I want to start by saying my godchild picked an orange off the tree in the backyard.

I want to start by saying as if it was a miracle.
~~~

~~~

I want to start by saying my old home on East Hill Road in Austerlitz.

I want to start by saying West Hill Road where my friend Hank taught my dog Flan to fish.

I want to start by saying that TC came over for dinner and we laughed.

I want to start by saying I felt loss and the fear of loss.

I want to start by saying when I told my mother that my divorce would soon be final, she choked and almost died.

I want to start by saying that risk has always meant a loss.
~~~

~~~

I want to start by saying we are meant to look at the light. And the space surrounding the light.

I want to start by saying R's folded gold sheet that now lies singular and isolated on some gallery or museum floor.

I want to start by saying the light on the gold and inside the fold changes throughout the day and night.

I want to start by saying something like fire.

I want to start by saying I once sat in R's studio, watching that gold sheet, for 24 hours.

I want to start by saying I tried to write everything I saw. The light as it changed during the day. The gold as it became bright and alive or quiet and dull.

I want to start by saying without context.
~~~

I want to start by saying who mined the gold and where are they.

I want to start by saying whose context, whose beauty.

I want to start by saying context matters.

I want to start by saying Alice Neel's apartment in New York.

I want to start by saying when I opened the kitchen cabinets to look for tea, an army of cockroaches crawled out. No living room separate from her studio and her paintings.

I want to start by saying Delmas's home in Truth or Consequences. No room separate from his studio and his paintings.

I want to start by saying my mother's home and her aspirations.

I want to start by saying why a house.

~~~

I want to start by saying that I lift my shirt to rub my chest as I wake up.

I want to start by saying a signal for my love to touch me.

I want to start by saying he does not notice.

I want to start by saying the clock and all the books.

I want to start by saying a dream.

I want to start by saying trees in the dawn.

I want to start by saying a forest beyond the windows.
~~~

I want to start by saying there is hardly a noise.

I want to start by saying my back to the door. Facing west.

I want to start by saying the reach of the mountains.

I want to start by saying I am now close to 15,141 words which equals 12 which equals 3.

Lucky.

NOTES

p. 22, Guibert, Hervé. *Ghost Image*, University of Chicago Press, 2014.

p. 68, *Shaker Heights, OH | Official website* (December 1, 2023). https://www.shakeronline.com/DocumentCenter/View/1733/Shaker-Heights-History-PDF.

p. 98, McClure, Michael. *Ghost Tantras*. City Lights / Grey Fox, 2013.

ACKNOWLEDGMENTS

Excerpts from this work have been previously published in *The Georgia Review*.

Thank you Caryl Pagel for your steady editorial brilliance, kindness, and reminders of home. Hilary Plum, Zach Peckham, Sevy Perez, Marlowe Jones, Joey Rooney, and Kristen Tetzmann for your careful reading and design which has allowed the physical object of this book to emerge with such beauty. Oliver Bendorf, Kaveh Akbar, Sarah Minor, Rebecca Brown, and Emerson Whitney for your hearts and friendship, for seeing this work so completely. To the loves with whom I can always start by saying all: Bob & Nan Tannenbaum, Johanna Skibsbrud, John Melillo, Olive & Sol, Rae Strozzo, TC Tolbert, Avery Wilde, Ariel Goldberg, Brian Blanchfield, John Myers, Susan Briante, Farid Matuk, Dorothy Varon, Eli Larriva, Sara Wenger, Joan Larkin. Grandmothers Rebecca Goldberg & Anna Tessler. Cousin Lois Grjebine. Cam Awkward-Rich, Franny Choi, CM Burroughs, Britt Billmeyer-Finn, Ames Hawkins, Duriel Harris, Soham Patel, CAConrad, Andrea Lawlor, Ari Banias, Dartricia Rollins, E.R. Anderson, Trace Peterson, Amy Martin, Jennifer DeClue, Margaret Groesbeck, Arthur Apostolou, Elliot Montague, Ren Hwang, Ocean Vuong. My early readers and guides, whose invaluable insights helped me navigate the formation of this work: Maureen Seaton, Sonny Nordmarken, Brian, John, Johanna, and the members of the Trans & Non-Binary writing group: Violet Spurlock, Lauren Levin, Syd Staiti, Jamie Townsend, Julian Talamantez Brolaski, Jos Charles, Zoe Tuck, Trish Salah, anise cinquepalmi, Noa Fields. Grateful to you all. To Julie Ezelle Patton and our mothers, the hands that have carried us.

The towns that have held me over the years – Decatur, GA; Austerlitz & New York, NY; Chéticamp & St. Joseph du Moine, NS; Cleveland, South Euclid, & Shaker Heights, OH; Easthampton, Florence, Northampton, & South Hadley, MA; Truth or Consequences, NM; and Tucson, AZ.

Your present is forever and now: Maureen. Victor. Isa.

RECENT CLEVELAND STATE UNIVERSITY POETRY CENTER PUBLICATIONS

edited by Caryl Pagel & Hilary Plum

POETRY

Mechanical Bull by Rennie Ament

World'd Too Much: The Selected Poetry of Russell Atkins
ed. Kevin Prufer and Robert E. McDonough

Advantages of Being Evergreen by Oliver Baez Bendorf

The Devil's Workshop by Xavier Cavazos

Ordinary Entanglement by Melissa Dickey

Dream Boat by Shelley Feller

My Fault by Leora Fridman

Orient by Nicholas Gulig

Twice There Was A Country by Alen Hamza

Age of Glass by Anna Maria Hong

outside voices, please by Valerie Hsiung

In One Form to Find Another by Jane Lewty

50 Water Dreams by Siwar Masannat

Mule: 10th Anniversary Edition by Shane McCrae

daughterrarium by Sheila McMullin

The Bees Make Money in the Lion by Lo Kwa Mei-en

Residuum by Martin Rock

Festival by Broc Rossell

Sun Cycle by Anne Lesley Selcer

Arena by Lauren Shapiro

Bottle the Bottles the Bottles the Bottles by Lee Upton

Innocence by Michael Joseph Walsh

No Doubt I Will Return A Different Man by Tobias Wray

ESSAYS

I Liked You Better Before I Knew You So Well by James Allen Hall

A Bestiary by Lily Hoang

Codependence by Amy Long

Telephone: Essays in Two Voices by Brenda Miller and Julie Marie Wade

The Leftovers by Shaelyn Smith

TRANSLATIONS

Almost Obscene by Raúl Gómez Jattin,
translated by Katherine M. Hedeen and Olivia Lott

Scorpionic Sun by Mohammed Khaïr-Eddine,
translated by Conor Bracken

I Burned at the Feast: Selected Poems of Arseny Tarkovsky,
translated by Philip Metres and Dimitri Psurtsev

for a complete list of titles visit CSUPoetryCenter.com